Soulful Journaling Guide

YOUR PATH TO HEALING AND SELF-DISCOVERY

Sending you love on your journey of healing and self-discovery!

Amanda Moser

AMANDA MOSER

SOULFUL JOURNALING GUIDE

Published by Amanda Moser, Moose Jaw, Canada

ISBN 0-978-1-77354-134-1

Publication assistance and digital printing in Canada by

PUBLISHING
PageMasterPublishing.ca

I wrote this book to help people find clarity in the truth of who they are, to have the courage to heal and live their lives from this truth. When I am sitting with my clients one-on-one, I feel so grateful that I get to be a vessel for messages of love and healing. I am also incredibly grateful I have the opportunity to be that same vessel for all who read this book. With guidance and love from the universe, may this journal help others connect to their souls.

- Amanda Moser

Contents

Introduction

Hi Friend!

Welcome to your new guide and journey to living a more soulful life! Each topic, question, and insight given in this journal was created just for you and guided from spirit. I have personally used these ways of journaling for many years now, and have also shared them with hundreds of other people across Canada to assist them as they heal and step into their personal power. I am so grateful for the fabulous coaches who have guided and encouraged me to get the pen down on the paper to connect with my soul. They helped teach me the right questions to ask, techniques to utilize and they reminded me of the importance of cultivating time with myself in order to positively affect all areas of my life. I am thrilled to have reached the point where I get to share with you all that I have learned along the way.

My name is Amanda Moser and I am an Intuitive Life Coach. I get incredibly excited to wake up and live each day. I love helping others heal and learn what living a more soulful life means to them. I work with clients on a one-on-one platform as well as through workshops, retreats, and online. I am a spiritual based coach and I use my abilities as a Psychic Medium to guide my clients to move beyond their current limiting belief patterns, reach their goals, and step into a life of freedom.

I am also a woman who isn't immune from the hardships of life. I have known what it feels like to be completely lost and unsure about where my life is headed. I have experienced depression, anxiety, loss of loved ones, estrangement from parents, a very low sense of self-worth, and have had my marriage fall apart. Additionally, I am a mom to two beautiful boys who are the loves of my life but who also give me a whole new level of life lessons. I have the utmost respect for my clients, the struggles they face, and the pain they experience. I understand things can sometimes seem hopeless or far out of reach. I have been there.

However, I also understand what it feels like to have that pull inside your heart to want better—the drive and determination to move forward despite how big the fears might be. I know the feeling of longing for a deeper self-love and awareness of who you really are inside, and the courage to actually show that person to the world. Every. Single. Day. I know the hard work it takes to change our old habits, heal our minds, and our bodies. I know how it feels when one day it seems like you can't get ahead or let go, and the next day it feels like so much has changed.

I didn't write any of these insights or questions for you without also knowing what it's like to have to work on them myself. The truth is that the journey of healing and growing never ends! I know I will never really perfect any of this—I'll simply deepen my awareness around it. So as you open these pages, I open my heart to you, and send you so much love and light as you move through this journey of discovery and healing. As you read these insights and write from your heart, please remember: *You are loved, you are safe, and you are always going to be a masterpiece and a work in progress simultaneously.*

It's time to begin. It's time to heal. It's time.

How To Use Your Journal

Journaling has a few different purposes and intentions. One of the intentions of journaling is to help you go deeper than the thoughts that keep spinning in your conscious mind. This is meant to help you connect with what is stored in your subconscious and your higher self. Your higher self is your soul. Journaling is also an effective way to release emotions that get stored in the body. Our emotions are energy and when we write them out it releases and shifts that energy. When we journal everyday it can be a great way to establish a healthy habit of connecting with our higher self and it can also create positive momentum in our life. Sometimes journaling is simply a way to align more with abundance and happiness by writing out what we are grateful for.

Your Journaling Process

One of the more common struggles people tell me they have with journaling is they don't know what to write about or how to go deeper into the writing. People tend to get caught up in their habit of overthinking instead of just letting the writing flow from a simple statement like, "today I am feeling…". It is important to remember that this writing is not for show. What you journal in these pages is for your eyes only and the more freedom you can give yourself, the better. Your writing does not have to contain proper grammar, punctuation, spelling, or even full sentences. Some of my clients share with me that they have so much going through their heads that all they can write at first are single words to help calm themselves enough to start putting sentences together.

This is your time to let yourself write out all the things you don't let yourself think because it might be "bad". It's not bad, you're just human. It is more beneficial for you to write it out and release it, or understand it better than to pretend those thoughts don't exist. It does not make you a negative person to be writing negative things. Writing and asking yourself the right questions afterwards can help you have a better understanding of the belief structure you have around the situation; this will help you decide how to move forward. It is also better to write and release the energy instead of allowing it to build in your body which will only cause anxiety, depression, pain, and other mental and physical health issues. This is your time to say all the things you want to say out loud but don't feel that you can… right now. Eventually you will get to the place where you will feel comfortable and confident enough to express your voice. You are finding it. You are refining it.

It can be helpful to intentionally move into state of relaxation before you begin journaling. Giving yourself thirty seconds to sit and breathe into your heart space before you start journaling can really help calm your mind and body. This will allow for an easier release of your thoughts and feelings. Begin by taking a deep breath in for a count of five and, as you do so, imagine the breath coming in through your heart space. Hold the breath for a count of three, and then exhale out your mouth for a count of five while you imagine the breath releasing through your heart space. Continue this for about thirty seconds. You will notice that your body starts to ground and relax.

Designated Time

Setting aside a special time of day to do your journaling will be incredibly helpful in creating momentum in your life. We sometimes fall back on habits of distracting and avoiding if we don't believe in the value of that connection time. In order to help us stay in what feels familiar and safe, our brains easily come up with excuses as to why we don't need to sit for those fifteen minutes to write. Deciding that this time with yourself is a priority is crucial to helping you live the life of your dreams.

I have had my own ups and downs in using journaling as part of my spiritual practice. There have been times that I have gone a couple of weeks without even touching it. I tried gentleness instead of self-sabotaging myself in those moments because accepting and loving myself was my goal. I tried to pay attention to how *not* journaling affected me. I explored what I was avoiding and how I was distracting myself. What I noticed was that I was more physically exhausted, anxious, unclear, and uninspired in my work—things just didn't seem to flow as nicely in my life when I stopped checking in with myself.

I have two little boys who are currently ages five and three, I run my own business, and generally have quite a busy schedule. Personal care has become important for me and I make sure to be mindful of slowing down and just being. A while ago, I started making it a priority to get up at 5:30am to sit and journal before my family woke up and the day took over. Right away I noticed that I had much more energy when I got up early for that connection time than I did when I chose to sleep in and miss it. I also find that playing meditation music while I journal or write helps me to focus and relax. I also enjoy having my morning hot lemon water or celery juice while I journal. These things help my body wake up and provide me with a feel good start to the day.

There will be a section in this journal that helps you explore what a spiritual practice looks like for you. Take notice of what helps motivate you to create a journaling time for yourself and an environment that feels good. Pick your favourite spot to write and find out what the best time of day is for you to sit down with your soul. What other things do you enjoy having with you in this time? Be curious. Allow the process to evolve as you do and know you can change it up whenever the need arises.

The Questions

Questions are essential when exploring our beliefs and the repetitive thoughts that support them. Some of these questions are provided for you in this journal, but they are based on the most likely scenario and are to help you practice. There will be times when the questions don't fully align with what you are writing and, as a result, you will need to adjust them so they apply more to you.

The most common and general question to ask yourself when writing is, "Why?" This can help take you deeper into the belief you may have around the situation and the patterns you have to support the belief. Questions that also support this can start with, "How...", "What...", and "When...".

Here are a few examples of the questions you might ask yourself:

I felt so irritated today. My husband did not pick up any of his things or do the dishes.

Why did I feel irritated?

Because I have asked him to do this 100 times and I hate that he gets lazy or thinks I will just do everything. I hate that I have to ask every time and he doesn't just do it on his own. I get so overwhelmed with all the things around the house.

Why is it important to me that he picks up after himself and does the dishes?

Because then I would feel like we are equal partners in this house. When he does those things, I feel valued and respected.

What can I do for myself right now to stand in my power and feel valued and respected?

I can tell him how important it is to me that he helps out around the house and what it makes me feel like when he doesn't. I can set boundaries with the things I do for him if he doesn't want to help me.

Some other questions you might be able to ask in this scenario are:

Do I feel like I deserve to be valued and respected?

When is another time in my life that someone has made me feel like I don't deserve to have help or speak up for what I need?

What kind of person does it make me if I have a dirty house? Do I want to continue to carry that belief? Why?

What do I really need right now to help ease my anxiety and stop feeling overwhelmed on a deeper level?

You are welcome to write directly in this book or in a separate book if you would like to reuse this again another time. You may find coming back to these questions later—after working on specific areas of your life—that you still can work on them, but you'll notice your awareness will have evolved.

Each section will have its own category or topic for you to explore. Each will start out with insights to help you have a deeper understanding of the topic, and your own personal journey and any healing that may be needed to help you move forward. If you have your own questions that come to you during your writing process, please trust this guidance and follow it. You do not always need to follow the guide exactly as it is written. You are your best guide. This book is meant to give you the confidence to start journaling on your own, all of the time. It is meant to teach you how to ask the right questions so you can deepen your awareness. It is what you need to heal so you can live a more soulful life.

Topics

Each of the topics chosen for this guide are based on the most common topics I discuss with my clients. Sometimes the topics might not initially seem relevant to your life. You might feel like you don't have any concerns or worries in a certain area. Try to allow yourself to explore with an open heart even if you feel this way. Sometimes you might discover something you weren't fully aware of, and sometimes it might simply increase your confidence in something you already knew for yourself.

Affirmations

You will find affirmations at the end of each section that will pertain to the topic of the section they are in. An affirmation is a positive statement that you can use to help you move beyond limiting thoughts and beliefs and into a more loving belief. When an affirmation is repeated several times, it can help reprogram your subconscious and support you in creating healthy habits that align with the new beliefs. Often times when an affirmation makes us feel uncomfortable, it is because it challenges an old belief structure; working with that affirmation can help us heal. Feel free to alter any of the affirmations in this guide so that they strongly resonate with you.

Some of the ways you can use your affirmations are by: writing them out, putting them on sticky notes throughout your house, making a vision board, using one as a screen saver on your phone, and reciting it with a Mala. Each time you see your affirmation, repeat it at least five times to yourself and try to breathe and feel it into your body. The number five holds the vibration of change and you will notice it feels different saying it at least five times instead of just once.

Book Recommendations

I will be sharing book recommendations periodically in this guide to provide more resources on certain topics should you need more support in a certain area. Some books will be repeated in a few sections because they can support you in more than one topic. I always recommend journaling while you read a book—allow yourself to explore with what is written in each chapter. How can you integrate what is being discussed into your life more? This helps you to be more engaged in the process of studying what is being shared and you will find that it will assist you in retaining information. If you don't feel drawn to any of the books shared in this guide, please do not feel discouraged. There are many authors and books out there on each of the topics discussed in this journal guide. These are simply the ones I have felt called to share.

Gratitude and Moments of Happiness

Reflecting on what we are grateful for and celebrating our moments of happiness helps us to stay in alignment with abundance and our soul's desires. I have made a point to have designated space in each section for this reflection time with yourself. When reflecting on moments of happiness try to think of even the simplest moments throughout your day as well as the big ones (if you have them). Celebrating a moment of happiness you had when listening to your children laughing, being greeted kindly by the clerk at the store, helping someone in need, giving a compliment, or watching a sunset, all help you to align with abundance. Feeling grateful for these big and small moments raises our vibration and helps to draw more of this abundance into your life!

Spiritual Practice

The way I define a spiritual practice is: a sequence of daily activities that people can do to support themselves in healing, personal growth, awareness, and connection. It is highly individual and can evolve as we do. It is important to have an awareness of our daily habits if we want to achieve our goals and become all that we are capable of becoming. Understanding ourselves is paramount to fulfilment.

I have intentionally placed this topic near the beginning of the book because it will create the foundation for everything you do moving forward. It will support you as you heal other areas of your life. You can continuously rediscover what this practice looks like for yourself as you move through life. It isn't something that you learn once and then leave off to the side; instead, you need to take it with you everywhere you go. It is important to make these activities a priority. When you choose daily habits that align with your soul you create more flow and ease in your day-to-day life. You will have more energy, clarity, feel more empowered to show up authentically, and attract more abundance and beautiful synchronicities.

I am not saying this process will always be easy to integrate, but it will definitely be worth it! Some of the things on my list take a lot of time and effort; however, ignoring them feels more detrimental. Consider this an investment and do your best to show up for yourself. I integrate practices that help me live my best life, and it pays dividends. You deserve love, healing, and joy in your life, too. We all deserve the best that life has to offer (and it has a lot to offer!)

I felt the best way to help you create your own spiritual practice was to break down activities into five very important categories. Those who have worked with me might be familiar with this practice as I am so passionate about sharing it. These five categories are: **Rest, Creativity, Nourishment, Play,** and

Connection. When I started my journey to healing, these are the five things I integrated into each day to help me connect with my soul and nourish my life. Now, I did not have the full awareness that I was doing this until almost two years in. I distinctly remember standing at my kitchen sink and asking my team to help me with inspiration on writing a new blog. Within seconds they showed me this list and all the fine details of how I had used it to shape my life into what it had become. I still focus on each of these things to this day!

So while there are many approaches to discovering your spiritual practice, this is the one I felt most called to share. Allowing yourself to focus on these areas of your life each day will help bring a sense of balance and nurturing to your mind, body, and soul. This section will begin by asking questions to help deepen your awareness to where you are currently at with any type of spiritual practice. Then it will move into exploring each of the five categories listed above. Try to have fun playing with some new ideas and activities that you can experience in this process. There is no pressure to do everything at once and it is ok to focus on adding one category at a time into your day. This is meant to help create more flow, not stress!

If you feel overwhelmed at the thought of integrating any of these activities, remember that it can feel uncomfortable at first when we are breaking old habits and creating new ones. Give yourself permission to move out of your comfort zone and embrace what this experience can teach you about yourself. Before you know it, you will be well on your way to understanding yourself on a deeper level and flowing through life with greater ease.

Let's Begin!

If I took all limitations and restrictions away, what would my ideal day look like? What activities would I be doing? Would I be spending it with anyone? What kinds of foods would I be eating?

_____

_____

_____

_____

_____

_____

_____

_____

_____

_____

_____

_____

When I close my eyes, take deep breaths, and imagine that entire day and all the fine details of it, what feelings do I notice in my body? Do I feel lighter, more relaxed, excited, happy, or content?

_____

_____

_____

_____

Do I want to feel these types of feelings more often? Why?

_____

_____

_____

_____

Do I currently prioritize time for myself every day?

If so, how?

_____

_____

_____

_____

If no, why not?

_____

_____

_____

_____

What activities or habits do I currently do each day that I enjoy?

_____

_____

_____

_____

Why do I enjoy them?

_____

_____

_____

_____

What activities or habits do I currently do each day that I don't enjoy?

_____

_____

_____

_____

What do I tell myself to justify continuing to participate in these things, even though I don't enjoy them?

_____

_____

_____

_____

_____

_____

Are my current beliefs around why I need to continue doing these unenjoyable things something I want to continue moving forward with in my life? Do these beliefs support me? Why or why not?

_____

_____

_____

_____

Beliefs are just stories we are told that we give meaning to, and carry throughout our lives. What is a new story I can create that would support me in making self-care a priority?

_____

_____

_____

_____

Where in my day can I make more time for self-care? What joyless activities can I eliminate to create more space for myself?

_____

_____

_____

_____

Do I believe that I will have more energy, inspiration, and love in my life if I change my habits? Why or why not?

_____

_____

_____

_____

What positive changes do I most want to see in my life if I integrate a spiritual practice?

_____

_____

_____

_____

In my own words, why is a spiritual practice important to me?

_____

_____

_____

_____

_____

With each of the five categories below, write beside them the possible activities you can do every day within that category. I will break down examples and more information on each category so you can have a better understanding of how to move forward with your writing and what it is you are looking to explore for yourself.

Rest: Taking a nap, going to bed earlier, having a bath, being mindful, or meditating.

Sometimes, if I have a busy schedule on a certain day, rest for me looks like taking 30 second mental breaks every hour. I set an alarm on my phone to go off every hour and then when I hear it ring, I take 30 seconds to breathe and pull myself into my body by focusing on all of my senses. I check in by noticing what colors I can see around me, how my body feels physically, what I can smell, if I can taste anything, and what I can touch (even if it's just the feeling of the ground under my feet or the texture of my clothing.)

Creativity: Crocheting, painting, writing, being creative with food or clothing, sewing, photography, scrapbooking, gardening, playing with playdoh, coloring, or decorating.

Creativity is like a vessel for your soul to shine through. When I connect to creative energy it feels like spirit in motion. Everyone is creative in some way; you just need to find which creative outlets bring you the most joy. It is important to take the expectations away from the final product. Focus on being present with the actual process of creation and the feelings of joy that it brings you. Notice any feelings of perfectionism or judgemental thoughts that might creep in. Stay in the awareness of the "why" behind what you are creating and the joy it brings you. This is especially important if you do a lot of creative type of work with your day-to-day job.

Notice your vulnerability in that moment of expressing your authenticity through creative energy; give it permission to come in. This is a beautiful opportunity to get more comfortable with what your authenticity looks like. When I feel called to make a new painting for myself, I set aside a couple of hours and make sure I won't be disturbed in that time. I lock myself in my little office, crank my music and just start painting. I never know what I am going to paint ahead of time, I just let my feelings speak to me and paint whatever vision that creates in my mind. Sometimes the result is random colors scattered across the canvas, other times it is a quote or a symbol. I do not worry about what it looks like; I simply want to enjoy the process.

Nourishment: This area is for you to focus on eating and nourishing your body with foods that feel good for you. This isn't a diet restriction, but a process of listening to your body and how it responds to what you eat. If you already have food you know your body loves and feels great about, then you can note these in this category.

Your body may need different foods to support it as it heals. You may find that you crave foods you used to avoid, or you may feel ill with foods you used to enjoy. It is also important to pay attention to your eating patterns. I was a neglectful eater and food was generally a last priority for me. Cooking would stress me out if I had too many other things on my to-do list. But I am also the worst hangry person you have ever met so I need food and I need it often. This combination used to result in me just eating what was convenient and not necessarily what my body needed. Once I started to explore this and heal where it stemmed from, I was able to be more mindful about taking time to eat the food my body required.

Play: Building sandcastles, making a snowman, playing at the park, playing fetch with your dog, and building forts.

We are born with the most instinctual ability to play. As we become adults we tend to disconnect with this part of ourselves as we get busy with the day-to-day things. Playing allows us to connect to our imagination which is a vital tool in creating a beautiful life. Our imagination is the essence of manifesting. Playing creates more flow, which means you feel lighter, happier, and you attract more synchronicities. Did you know that one of the quickest and most effective ways to raise your vibration at any given moment is to dance? It is also very playful!

We tend to struggle so much as adults with allowing ourselves to be playful and to not take life so seriously. Try to imagine what you loved doing as a child and how you could give yourself permission to engage in that kind of play now. If you have young children of your own, let them lead the way and get down to their level to see the world from their perspective. Allow yourself to explore your imagination and feel the healing that laughter brings.

Connection: This category is such an essential piece to my day! Connecting to the soul helps us to better navigate nourishing the mind and body, which is why I find it to be so important. Connection can be achieved through certain types of intentional meditations, yoga, prayer, consistent acts of mindfulness, meditative walks in nature, soulful conversations with other likeminded people, inspirational shows or podcasts, volunteering, and journaling. Journaling, if you hadn't noticed, is my favourite! When your connection time involves other people, it is good to have some designated reflection time afterward. This really helps clarify the awareness you may have had during the period of connection.

These five categories help nourish us in a balanced way by connecting us with our mind, body, and soul which is optimal for growth.

Fill in your own examples of what activities you feel drawn to…

Rest:

_____

_____

_____

_____

_____

Creativity:

_____

_____

_____

_____

_____

Nourishment:

_____

_____

_____

_____

Play:

_____

_____

_____

_____

Connection:

_____

_____

_____

_____

Sometimes you can combine two of the categories into one activity. For example, you can be creative with your food by trying a new recipe and playing with the colors in the ingredients. The key is to be present and mindful of the process. If you are creating a recipe, but you are thinking of 30 other things (that have nothing to do with the recipe itself) while you make it, then you will miss out on the fun of making something new. You won't enjoy the end result as much because you weren't fully present for the process.

The next part of these activities is the process of listening to your body or, another way of saying it, your intuition. Each day you can check in to see how you want to nourish your creative side, and then you imagine yourself doing each of the activities you have written down in the creativity category.

Whichever activity sparks a feeling of excitement, lightness, or peacefulness in your body is the one you focus on for the day. Sometimes you will find that you feel drawn to the same activity for a long stretch of time before wanting to try something different. There is nothing wrong with this—it is good to practice trusting your intuition. Honing your intuition this way will come in handy when dealing with the bigger or more emotional decisions in life.

From here you can create a schedule if you find it easier to manage your time and activities. For example, if you want to make sure you get up earlier to go for a walk every morning, or have a yoga practice before bed, you can set a repeating reminder in your phone, organizer, or write a physical note-to-self. Anything that supports you in keeping up your routine will be beneficial for sustainability. This is a very flexible process that you can maneuver, in whatever way you need, to make it work for you and your life. Soon you will find more balance and feel a deeper sense of wholeness in your life!

Affirmations

My wellbeing is a priority.

I am deserving of care and love.

I am divinely guided and connected.

I am supported by others as I support myself.

Book Recommendations

The Power of Now by Eckhart Tolle

The Happiness Project by Gretchen Rubin

Gratitude

Today I am grateful for:

_____

_____

_____

_____

_____

_____

_____

Moments of Joy

Today's moments of joy:

_____

_____

_____

_____

_____

_____

_____

_____

_____

Limiting Beliefs

Limiting beliefs are stories or programs that live in our subconscious mind that we carry throughout our lives. They dictate our responses and thoughts to situations and people. They feel sincere and very real but generally disconnect us from the truth of our soul, which in itself is limitless energy. They test our faith, belief in ourselves, and trust in the universe. They can limit our perceptions and understanding of ourselves and others.

Understanding our limiting beliefs and how to move beyond them is vital in healing all areas of our lives. If we can't move beyond our perceptions and the stories we currently tell ourselves, then we won't be able to create a new reality. In each section you will notice that certain questions help you better understand the limiting thoughts you have regarding that specific area of your life.

This section will help you dive deeper into your current belief structures, learn how to find the root of them, and figure out how to move beyond them. Limiting beliefs are a continuous process of healing. Once you think you have it in the bag, something else comes up to deepen your awareness even more. This does not mean you are doing anything wrong if, later on in life, something shows up that you thought you had already worked on. Your soul cannot move backwards; it is endlessly evolving. Each situation is simply expanding your awareness and creating more depth of understanding. You always have the option to embrace each situation as a new learning experience for yourself and face it head on.

Since limiting beliefs are limiting perceptions, they close us off to seeing the potential solutions to our struggles. They greatly support a victim mentality and keep us out of alignment from the abundance that is readily available to us. Some people would call these "blocks in your energy". For example, the statement "I am too emotional" closes us off from understanding how expressing our emotions keeps them from building in our body and hurting us physically and mentally, or blinds us from seeing how our vulnerability can inspire others. It keeps us focusing on lack and weakness instead of the incredible strength there is from expressing how we feel. It puts us in the space of carrying other people's insecurities and allowing them to dictate how we perceive ourselves.

You can start being aware of your limiting beliefs by looking for common ways you speak about yourself and your life. When you are using phrases such as: "I should be...", "I have to...", "That doesn't come easy for me!", or "I have such bad luck!" you can be sure that these are good indicators of where you are currently limiting yourself in your life.

Here are some other common limiting thoughts:

- I am not smart enough

- I can only make money by...

- I can't do that because I am a woman

- I am too much for them

- I need to do this so that person will love me

- I have depression and anxiety so I can't do that

- People will forever see me for the mistakes I made in the past

- I will only be healthy if I eat certain foods and do a certain amount of exercise

- I won't be happy until I am in a relationship

- I have to do this to fit in or I won't have any friends

- If I set that boundary then I will never make any new friends

- I can't have a job like that because it's not a "real" job

- No one will ever love me

- I will never heal from this

- I will never be successful at that

- No one will support me

- I can never get ahead with money

- I won't be happy until you're happy

- I am incapable

- I don't deserve to be loved

- I am not enough until I have…

- I need to sacrifice myself for this

- I can't let my walls down or I will get hurt

- I can't share my opinion on that because they will judge me

These are not all of the limiting thoughts, but it does give you an idea of what they are in order to start recognizing them in your own life.

The most common places that our limiting beliefs can stem from are society, our parents (generational patterns), traumatic experiences, other relationships, and religious teachings. Remember that everyone is doing the best they can in their life, but we still have a choice to break patterns that are no longer serving us as we become aware of them.

As our self-worth grows, so does our belief that we can have better and do better for ourselves! Limiting beliefs can take a fair bit of time to work through, depending on how strongly we give them significance, and they require the assistance of many other areas of our healing in order for us to move beyond them. So please be gentle with yourself as you move through this process and know that you will get there—one step at a time!

So how do we heal our limiting beliefs? In other words, how do we change these thought patterns into new thoughts that are more aligned with our soul? We can start by becoming aware of what the limiting thought is and where it came from. This is not saying you are to go back into a painful memory and re-live it. You have been there once and you don't need to live it over again in order to take what you need from it. The awareness of where the belief came from helps to kill its power and the truth we believe it carries.

When we start to see that the belief itself was just something someone told us, believing it as the only truth, then we do not need to feel so attached to it. We can start to create a new story or belief that feels lighter to our body and helps us move forward in a way that feels good to our hearts. Sometimes the limiting belief comes from something we told ourselves after experiencing pain. We create the belief in our mind to be true in order to validate the experience and sometimes to try and avoid it from happening again. When we can heal from the experience itself by honouring our feelings, opening our hearts to forgiveness, and putting the significance into the lesson instead of the pain, then we can move forward without continuously harming ourselves from that experience.

Talking to someone with a third party perspective can help you get clearer on what your limiting thoughts might be. It is not easy for anyone to see a pattern they are stuck in, and having someone ask you the right questions to see a different perspective can be very beneficial in helping you see how to move forward in a new energy.

It can also sometimes be difficult to let go of an old limiting thought if we have created an identity around the pain attached to it. Sometimes we simply don't know who we are outside of our pain and limitations. The fear of the unknown is often enough to keep us from feeling motivated to create concrete change. The limiting patterns sometimes feel better than the freedom, simply because they are familiar. Finding and creating support for yourself is vital in situations like this.

You will need many gentle reminders to focus on the new thought patterns in order to get more comfortable with the idea of them and to live your life truly believing them. Sticky notes are one great way to do this. If you take a limiting thought and counter it with a positive thought, you can put it on a sticky note somewhere in your house where you will see it often. You will want it to be at eye level and easy to catch your attention. Remember to move them around so that you don't get too comfortable with them in one spot and stop noticing them altogether.

Let's begin your personal discovery into how you can live a more limitless life!

From the list of limiting beliefs written above, which ones currently resonate with me in my life?

_____

_____

_____

_____

Are there any limiting beliefs I am aware of that are not on the list? If yes, what are they?

_____

_____

_____

Who or what do I feel influenced my limiting beliefs?

_____

_____

_____

_____

Which of the limiting beliefs on my list do I feel affects me the most right now?

_____

_____

_____

When is my earliest memory of someone, or a certain situation, making me feel this way?

_____

_____

_____

_____

What emotions do I feel when remembering this person or situation?

_____

_____

_____

_____

What other negative thoughts do I have about myself when I think about this memory?

_____

_____

_____

_____

Can I be open to the process of forgiving myself, the other person, or the situation that caused this belief?

_____

_____

If I don't feel ready, what is something I can do to help myself become ready?

_____

_____

_____

_____

Is there something I am afraid of knowing about myself or uncovering about my life if I allow myself to move forward from this?

_____

_____

_____

What lessons can I take away from the experience to positively influence how I move forward?

_____

_____

_____

_____

Can I accept who I am in this moment, as the person creating a new way of living life? Why or why not?

_____

_____

_____

_____

Can I accept who I was in that moment where the situation or person affected how I then perceived my life? Why or why not?

_____

_____

_____

_____

What can I do to show myself appreciation and love for all that I am right now?

_____

_____

_____

_____

Why do I want to show myself this love?

_____

_____

_____

_____

_____

There is always a limitless and positive belief that helps us move beyond a limiting one. For example, "I never get ahead with money" can be countered with, "Money is energy and I am open to aligning with the abundant prosperity of the universe!" What are the limitless beliefs that counter your list of limiting ones you wrote above?

_____

_____

_____

_____

_____

What daily habits can I enforce to support myself moving forward, help me heal, and create this new belief as reality for me?

_____

_____

_____

_____

Do I feel I will be supported moving forward as I try to implement these new beliefs? Why or why not?

_____

_____

_____

_____

How can I ask for more support if I don't currently feel supported?

_____

_____

_____

Do I want to move forward regardless of having support or not? Why or why not?

_____

_____

_____

Affirmations:

I allow the freedom of my soul to guide me.

I am open to new ways of living.

It is safe for me to move forward.

I am supported as I heal.

Book Recommendations:

The Untethered Soul by Michael Singer

Wishes Fulfilled by Wayne Dyer

You Can Heal Your Life by Louise Hay

Gratitude

Today I am grateful for:

_____

_____

_____

_____

_____

_____

Moments of Joy

Today's moments of joy:

_____

_____

_____

_____

_____

_____

_____

_____

Speaking Your Truth

Speaking our truth is when we unashamedly allow our hearts to guide every move we make and every word we speak—regardless of how we were taught growing up or the beliefs of anyone we currently share our life with. In this space, we are not speaking with bitterness and we are not trying to prove ourselves; rather, we are coming from a space of love for everyone. This is not saying that we go against everyone and everything we were taught. This is saying you take what works for you and leave the rest.

Allowing ourselves the freedom to speak freely about who we are as individuals, to absolutely anyone, can be incredibly difficult to achieve. Right from childhood we are told to never talk back and to raise our hand to ask permission to speak in class. Now, both of these "rules" were taught with good intentions of teaching respect for others. However, somewhere along the line, our perceptions of these types of rules became quite strong. They began making us feel wrong or bad about speaking up if we did not align with what we were being told. If the people enforcing the rules had a sense of fear attached to them (from their own insecurities) then this could have greatly affected how we perceived them.

As a child, if you were given consequences for "bad" behaviour but you tried to explain yourself and were punished more because your words were perceived as talking back or being difficult, then you would start to associate pain with speaking your truth. Children can also disconnect from their truth if they feel pain by being made fun of for their interests. For example, imagine you were given an assignment in class to write an essay on someone you admired and you chose Leonardo da Vinci. You selected him not only for his incredible ability to create various types of art and inventions, but also because you felt strongly about creating. Now, imagine the other kids in your class picked people who played a sport or chose their parents, and they simply could not relate to you for your love of history and desire to be a creative person, so they mocked you. This could make you, as a child or young adult, feel quite insecure about your passions in life and, in turn, feel wrong for loving these things. At this young age, it would be hard to see that people only resorted to mocking you because they didn't understand you.

Even as adults certain situations can really affect how we feel when it comes to simply voicing our likes and dislikes. If you were raised in a home that followed Catholicism, but as an adult you feel strongly that their values or beliefs aren't right for you, then it might be hard to voice this to your family if it is something that is very important to them. You might feel that they will lose sight of who you are as an individual and feel you need to prove that you are a good person.

If we notice any of these patterns as adults then we have the incredible opportunity to break free from these perceptions and live in a more soulful way. If you can begin to look at the experiences that made you feel small or insignificant as moments that were building a strong foundation for your future, then you can start to create something truly amazing from it. What I mean by foundation is, if you didn't experience moments in life where you felt your voice was insignificant, then would you fully be able to feel the value in speaking your truth? If you have to work to move beyond a perceived obstacle and stand in who you are, then you are more likely to truly appreciate living from this space, and you will be less likely to allow anyone to influence you otherwise.

We are also given the incredible opportunity to experience what it means to unconditionally love someone. Although we are all one because we all come from the same source energy, we are not all the same. Our differences allow us to learn what it means to love people without needing them to be the same. This allows us to hold space for them better, and to feel more comfortable being our authentic selves. We have an opportunity to move into a more divine space where we see that everyone and everything is happening in a divine order; that we are all guided and our experiences are here to help us collectively evolve; that there is no right or wrong way to live, only what is right for you. Your truth is exactly what the world needs. I call this trusting the flow of life. When you speak your truth and follow your heart, it is always for everyone's highest good.

Another opportunity we have is to step into the understanding that we are not responsible for how other people feel. This can be a hard one for people to sit with and understand because it shows up in so many areas of our day-to-day lives; it can take some time to implement. First, I will say that this understanding does not remove our responsibility of being considerate of others. We are moving into a space of more divine love so it is important to consider others and how our actions might affect them. This *is* love. However, if my feelings were hurt by the actions of someone else and I keep looking at them throughout the entire healing process, focusing on what they are or aren't doing to make it right, then it takes away the responsibility I have to look at what is right for me or how I could make things right for myself. It keeps me in a victim mentality and unable to clearly see how I could grow from the experience. If we are always stopping ourselves from doing what feels right for our hearts because we are afraid of how others will feel, then we are not serving them or ourselves... nobody is benefitting. We cannot control how other people perceive life, not even our children. All we can do is act in love and move forward in a way that feels good to our souls.

How much you struggled to speak your truth will affect how you move to the beautiful space of unconditional love and understanding for everyone. A pattern I saw in myself, and in so many of my clients, was that once they started the process of speaking up and living more authentically, they would easily be agitated by people who didn't understand or they struggled to continue having relationships with them. I labeled this the "temper tantrum phase" and I started calling it this for myself because I felt like I went from not having a voice of my own, to the other extreme of not wanting to back down and feeling resentful towards people who spoke against me. In my mind, I thought they were all wrong for not seeing things my way or not instantly accepting me. It resembled the pattern that a lot of people have of judging people for judging them. After a while, I started to calm down and feel more confident in my voice. This confidence became like a gentle stillness and needed zero validation from anyone, but not in a bitter way. I no longer needed validation and I accepted other people's voices too.

Be gentle with yourself through this process and please don't expect to jump to the space of unconditional love right away. I believe the reason I am able to stand more in the gentle confidence space is because I first had to learn how to honour my voice and all of my feelings that came up in the process. I did not feel I needed to prove anything because I developed a trust in myself through this process of honouring, a trust that I will care for myself and do what feels right for my heart— regardless of other people's thoughts and opinions. I am enough and I am worthy!

Often people do not know how to begin speaking their truth because they don't actually know what it is. They have spent so much of their lives living to please others as their core coping mechanism that they really do not know any other way to live. This will take some time. Your thoughts, interests, and perceptions will change throughout your life so please do not feel bound to one way forever. Embrace the process of evolving as you honour yourself each step of the way. Let's start getting to know who you are and how you can begin shining that amazing light of yours for the world to see. I promise that there are people out there who cannot wait to love you in all of your beautiful authenticity. Please take your time with these questions, and remember not to limit yourself or filter what you write. You are perfect just the way you are!

What is it like to be me?

_____

_____

_____

_____

_____

_____

_____

_____

_____

_____

_____

As I wrote the story of what it is like to be me, how did I feel?
Why did I feel this way?

_____

_____

_____

_____

If I took all limitations away and could re-write that story, how
would I write it?

_____

_____

_____

_____

_____

_____

Do I feel afraid to live my life with the new narrative I just
wrote? Why or why not?

_____

_____

_____

_____

Am I willing to make changes that will help me feel ready to live my life more closely to the new story? If yes, why? If no, why not?

_____

_____

_____

_____

What are my likes and dislikes when considering foods, activities, political views, spiritual or religious beliefs, clothing, and any other things that might come to mind?

_____

_____

_____

_____

_____

_____

_____

_____

_____

_____

_____

_____

Are there any of my likes and dislikes that I struggle to openly share with people? Which ones, and why?

_____

_____

_____

When was a prominent time in my life that I felt I could not speak my truth? Why do I feel I could not show up authentically at that time?

_____

_____

_____

_____

_____

Do I feel that I often resort to people pleasing? If yes, what am I afraid of in those moments? If no, what thoughts do I have that keep me from doing this?

_____

_____

_____

_____

_____

_____

Who did I want to impress the most in my life when I was a child? Why?

_____

_____

_____

_____

_____

_____

Who do I currently want to impress the most in my life? Why?

_____

_____

_____

_____

_____

Do I believe these people would have loved me (or will continue to love me) if I allowed them to see the most authentic version of who I am? Why or why not?

_____

_____

_____

_____

_____

_____

Is there something I have always wanted to do in my life but haven't done because I am afraid of what others will think of me? What is it? What am I afraid they will think or do if I followed through with it?

_____

_____

_____

_____

_____

How do I wish I could feel in my closest relationships? Why?

_____

_____

_____

_____

_____

_____

How do I wish I could feel and act in new social situations? Why?

_____

_____

_____

_____

What changes can I start making today that will help me start living more authentically?

_____

_____

_____

_____

Do I believe I deserve to live a life that is free of other people's expectations? Why or why not?

_____

_____

_____

_____

Do I believe that people's expectations of me are just symptoms of their perception of their own lives? Why or why not?

_____

_____

_____

_____

Do I believe that I am responsible for how other people feel? Why or why not?

_____

_____

_____

_____

_____

Am I willing to take complete ownership of my life and realize that I am the only person I can control or have power over? Why or why not?

_____

_____

_____

_____

If I showed up every day as the person I am behind closed doors, do I believe I will be supported and loved? Why or why not?

_____

_____

_____

_____

Is there someone who stands out the most when it comes to silencing my voice? Who are they and how did they make me feel I could not speak my truth?

_____

_____

_____

_____

_____

Am I willing to be open to forgiving this person? Can I believe they were doing the best they could with what they knew? Do I feel this dismisses my feelings? Why or why not?

_____

_____

_____

_____

_____

_____

_____

Affirmations

It is safe for me to speak my truth.

I am loved and supported as my authentic self.

I am beautiful.

I am enough.

I deserve to be loved.

I trust my heart to lead the way.

My voice matters.

Books

Warrior Goddess Training by Heather-Ash Amara

The Four Agreements by Don Miguel Ruiz

Light Is the New Black by Rebecca Campbell

Gratitude

Today I am grateful for:

_____

_____

_____

_____

_____

_____

_____

Moments of Joy

Today's moments of joy:

_____

_____

_____

_____

_____

_____

_____

_____

_____

Connecting To Your

Inner Child

Connecting to our inner child is connecting to the part of us that holds such innocence and pure divine energy. Our inner child still lives on, parallel to who we are now. It is important to nurture the child inside of us and open ourselves up to allowing her love and innocence to shine through. Our inner child is an incredible guide to help us know where we currently need healing in our lives.

To help create more ease while reading this section, I will be using she or her to describe your inner child, instead of her/his or she/he each time.

We all experienced some level of pain or trauma as children that created the starting point of some unhealthy patterns, or patterns that disconnected us from our truth—whether it was being left out of group activities at school, watching your parents get a divorce, or being told not to cry. Before these experiences, we were living freely and without worry, but afterwards they began to cloud and change our perceptions of who we are.

Do you ever notice how young children can stay tuned into their imagination and create play all day long? For them, almost every moment is an opportunity to explore. Just the other day I watched my two young boys, with wondering eyes, as they turned the waiting room of the doctor's office into a big, beautiful mountain scene, just by using their imaginations. They described the cave they were hiding in, in the mountain, which was actually the side table between the chairs. The adult in me wanted to tell them to sit nicely on the chairs but the table was plastic and they weren't bothering anyone, so I tried to simply enjoy their adventure as they told it to me like a story.

You were that child once too! At one time in your life you had the capacity to imagine anything you wanted and play all the time without any anxiety whatsoever. You still have the capacity to be carefree; it is your perception that is often clouded. It is concerned with to-do lists, expectations, rules, and stories of what an adult is supposed to look and act like.

You can nurture your inner child in various ways. One powerful method is talking kindly to her and giving her the love she always desired. Mirror work is great for this! Talking to yourself in the mirror as if you are talking to your inner child, and gently rubbing your stomach like you would a baby, can be very soothing. You can also nurture this young girl by giving her permission to live through you now by playing and using your imagination freely.

Allowing your inner child to guide you to the areas of the self that need healing can be very effective. She helps you get directly to the starting point of a lot of the habits and limiting thoughts that have consumed your life. Healing these areas is nurturing to your inner child because she is a parallel energy to who you are now.

In the questions to follow, we will be going through two different processes of awareness. The questions will help you rediscover the beautiful energy of your inner child that will allow her to shine in your present life. You will also be taken through a journaling process that helps you alternately connect to your conscious and subconscious mind.

Your subconscious mind has stored all of the answers from your inner child. Your conscious mind will be asking the questions and your subconscious mind will be answering them. Your dominant hand is your conscious mind and your non-dominant hand is your subconscious mind. You will ask the questions while writing with your dominant hand and answer them using your non-dominant hand. I will be writing out the questions ahead of time, but you will need to rewrite them in order to create an authentic dialogue with your inner child.

Chances are that the answers you write with your non-dominant hand will be illegible but please do not stress over this part. All that matters is staying in the flow of energy that is created with the conversation.

In order to help you let go of trying to overthink or control what is being written by your subconscious mind, I suggest that you take five minutes to breathe into your body and relax before this writing practice. Allowing yourself to journal for a while about how you are feeling, or what might be weighing on your mind before this activity, will help you get centered and remove any heavy thoughts. Answering the other questions in this section can be helpful as well if you do them right before the subconscious writing. Doing this will aid in connecting to your inner child and relaxing into the writing process.

The practice of connecting to your inner child through a conversation between the conscious and subconscious minds is usually not an activity that needs to be done all of the time. However, if you are feeling bogged down with emotions or unclear of how to move forward in a situation, this type of journaling is not only beneficial, it is likely something you need. I have had many clients who have found clarity with this writing practice after expressing to me that they were feeling stuck in their life, but they were not really sure why.

People often find that this exercise gives them clarity because it shows them what they need in their life right now. For example, the first time I tried this type of journaling, my inner child took me back to the age of three. She said she was hiding in the closet in her room, waiting for someone to come find her and give her attention. As I wrote these words with my non-dominant hand I could see the image of my mom in the kitchen, my infant sister in a little chair on the floor next to her, and my dad in the garage. My inner child told me she was sad and felt like no one cared about her because they didn't notice she was "missing". Until I wrote this, I had completely forgot that I used to hide in the closet for attention as a child! It led me to ask myself: "How do I look for validation and attention now as an adult?" I did not see this as a pattern until I had done this type of journaling; it gave me an opportunity to explore this part of myself and step into a new depth of self-worth.

Allow your inner child to guide you towards living a more playful and free life by connecting to and nurturing her as part of your regular practice. Let's begin to explore how the wonderful energy of your inner child can begin to shine in your everyday life!

What were my favourite toys and activities as a child?

_____

_____

_____

_____

_____

_____

When I go back into a memory of playing with my favourite toy or doing my favourite activity, how do I remember feeling?

_____

_____

_____

_____

How can I incorporate these activities into my life now?

_____

_____

_____

_____

Do I make stories or attach to a story that says I cannot do these activities anymore? If yes, what is the story and why do I feel bound to it?

_____

_____

_____

_____

What is something I did as a child that made me feel free?

_____

_____

_____

_____

How can I incorporate this activity into my life now?

_____

_____

_____

_____

Why do I feel it is important to nurture and connect to my inner child?

_____

_____

_____

_____

How do I wish I was loved when I was a child?

_____

_____

_____

_____

How was I loved and nurtured in ways that felt good to my heart?

_____

_____

_____

_____

Did I feel any anger or resentful feelings come up when I answered the last two questions? If yes, who are these emotions directed at? Have these feelings created perceptions of my childhood that block me from seeing the ways I was loved and cared for? Why or why not?

_____

_____

_____

_____

If I could sit down with my five-year-old self, what advice would I give her?

_____

_____

_____

_____

Do I feel that my advice was coming from a place of defensiveness or resentment? Why or why not?

_____

_____

_____

What kind and loving words can I speak to my inner child when I stand in front of the mirror?

_____

_____

_____

_____

Meditation Practice

Take five minutes to sit quietly and breathe deeply into your stomach. Feel your feet grounding into the earth and give yourself permission to be here in this moment. Feel your body sinking deeper into your seat with each exhale. Once you are relaxed, welcome your inner child to this moment with you, and say hello. Continue with nice relaxed breathing and ask your inner child, "What do you need? How can I love you more?" Check in with your body and make sure it is still nice and relaxed.

Allow yourself to sit in this moment without expectations while you wait for your inner child to show you what she needs. It may take some time to receive any messages and you will need to trust your intuition with what comes forward. She might show you what she needs in ways of memories, colors, foods, words, feelings, smells, and more. Allow the answers to come forward without judgement. If you feel you did not receive any answers, try to revisit this practice frequently until something does come forward for you as it may take time for you to relax and hear what your inner child wants to say.

Write all of the messages your inner child shared with you:

_____

_____

_____

_____

_____

_____

_____

Moving forward, what can I do to nurture my inner child in the ways she showed me during the meditation?

_____

_____

_____

_____

_____

Subconscious Journaling

The following questions will be written with your dominant hand (conscious mind). You will answer each question with your non-dominant hand (subconscious mind) in order to create a conversation with your inner child. You will need to write the questions yourself rather than simply answering them with your non-dominant hand—this helps you stay connected to the energy of your inner child. Once your inner child has answered the final question, you will want to remind her, in your own words, that she is an adult now and you will love and care for her.

Hi (first name).

How old are you?

What are you doing?

How are you feeling?

Using what your inner child showed you in this journaling practice, how does this reflect who you are now and how you respond to life?

_____

_____

_____

_____

_____

How would you like to feel and/or respond differently moving forward?

_____

_____

_____

_____

_____

What new habits can you create to help instil these feelings?

_____

_____

_____

_____

_____

Affirmations

I am in control of how I feel.

I have all that I need.

I am worthy of being loved and cared for.

I am enough.

I give myself permission to heal and step into a new way of being.

I am playful.

I am happy.

It is safe for me to show my silly and fun side.

I accept my past and embrace my future.

Book Recommendations

The Awakened Family by Shefali Tsabary, Ph.D.

Wishes Fulfilled by Wayne Dyer

Gratitude

Today I am grateful for:

_____

_____

_____

_____

_____

_____

_____

_____

Moments of Joy

Today's moments of joy:

_____

_____

_____

_____

_____

_____

_____

_____

Relationships

Each section of this guide could be its own book because there is so much to discover within the topics. Specifically, this is a journey of self-discovery and, most importantly, it is about living authentically. As such, we are going to look at how you show up authentically in your relationships and how you can heal and thrive in them. What I want you to remember is that the relationship you have with yourself is the most important of all as this will affect all of your outside relationships.

Our relationships really do mirror to us almost everything we need to know about how to break free from our own limitations and accept who we are. The struggle is learning to be aware and allowing the process to happen without an immense amount of fear taking over. These fears can often show themselves in the expectations we have for the people we share our lives with, mainly our parents, spouses, siblings, and children. We battle with fears of being alone, speaking our truth, and setting boundaries. But regardless of how big our fears may be. The loving essence of our souls is much bigger.

As you move into a more divine space of authenticity, it is important to remember that all of us are beautiful souls. Despite any human faults, we are all guided for our collective evolution. If you can move into a space of trusting yourself and trusting your relationships to help you grow, then it can be much easier to accept what they were, and what they are today. When you can accept them then you can embrace the lessons they are bringing you, along with the love that is here for you.

This growth can also mean that you start to create boundaries out of love for everyone and not just to defend and protect yourself. Can you feel the difference in the energy when you read that? Standing in boundaries out of love for everyone carries a very different energy than standing in boundaries from a place of defensiveness, resentment, and protection. You may also find that you need fewer boundaries when you completely love and accept who you are. When you take more responsibility for your own energy and how you feel then it takes the focus away from needing to protect yourself so much. You won't feel as drained around certain people or social situations when you allow people to simply be who they are without expectations.

When you are in the space of needing to protect yourself then your focus is on the energy you don't want, which will only pull it in more. However, you will feel less drained if you concentrate on bringing love to each room and personal encounter—love for yourself and each soul— without needing people to be different than who they are in order to make you feel more comfortable. When your focus is on love, you will attract more love! When you stand in this space you are more likely to see when something isn't serving you or the other person. You will realize when you are enabling someone to stay stuck in an old pattern by not moving forward yourself.

This does not mean we heal strictly for the purpose of helping someone else because we cannot control anyone's perceptions; after all, they may not do what you want in the end anyway. This means you heal for yourself and that will, in turn, shift the energy and give the other people involved a chance to grow as well. All we can do in these moments is hold space and give them the freedom to move forward in whatever way is right for their soul.

A large struggle people have with setting boundaries is fear of how the other person will react, the fear that they will hurt that person or make them angry. This can cause people to have an inner dialogue that tells them they are bad or wrong if the other person reacts in these ways, or it can trigger the dialogue that is already there. However, when you expand your awareness to a bigger picture, you can see that when you don't set the boundary then you are continuing the cycle of pain for yourself and the other person. Your resentment will continue to build and eventually the relationship will end leaving you with a fair bit of work to do to release all of that anger.

I always describe boundaries as something that will speed up the inevitable. If the relationship is meant to continue, then the boundary will help you both move forward together in a way that feels better to your heart. If the relationship is not meant to continue (at the current moment in time) then the boundary will help to end it and also end the cycle of energy you were in during that time. This does not mean you cannot have a relationship with that person ever again; it is simply breaking the cycle of energy. Sometimes something breaks the energy cycle you are in and the relationship can be maintained during the shift, for example: the death of a mutual loved one, an affair, a change in career, or time apart. Sometimes people spend time apart and heal in ways that help their souls realign later on. There is no right or wrong to how these processes unfold—it is simply what your soul chooses in this life to help you evolve.

I often hear people talk about setting boundaries but they weren't effective, the other person didn't respect the boundary they set in place. This largely has to do with how you stand in the energy of the boundary itself. If you tell someone you won't tolerate something anymore but do not enforce what it means if that person continues their actions, then they can feel that energy and don't take the boundary seriously. There is no consequence for them if they continue and the situation so far has shown them that this is true. How you stand in your self-worth will greatly affect how you enforce your boundaries. If you do not believe you deserve better than the current circumstances then it will be easier to allow people to walk on you. Be gentle with this process and know that it takes time. As you work on all other areas of your healing and self-discovery, the necessary boundaries will be easier to put in place.

We walk this line of knowing that we are not responsible for other people's perceptions while simultaneously working together to create healthy relationships where each person feels valued and respected. This belief expands even more into the knowing that we can't hurt people. This is sometimes hard for people to sit with because it goes against many programs, so let's break it down a bit more.

If we cannot control other people's perceptions then we cannot be responsible for how they feel and, in turn, we cannot hurt them. The same situation with two different people could result in very different responses. For example, if you tell a couple of friends you have to cancel your plans for dinner at the last minute because you are drained from work, one friend might completely understand and thank you for being honest whereas the other friend might be upset that you were inconsiderate of their time and wished you followed through on things. The fact is, we cannot hurt people because we cannot control how they perceive life. This does not take away our responsibility of being considerate of others and having conversations with them if they do get hurt. It simply means everyone has an opportunity to look at themselves first in order to see what they need to do for themselves before coming together to work on the relationship and support each other.

Relationships evolve as we do and we draw in relationships that align with our current energy. This means that if you want better in a relationship, then you need to align with the energy of the relationship you want—the current relationship could continue and evolve as you do, or it could end and make room for one that aligns with the energy you have moved into. How you view yourself and your actions will be good indicators of what your relationships will look like.

It is only possible to allow others to love us to the capacity that we love ourselves. You will not recognise love the same way if it is beyond what you believe you deserve. You can tell yourself things like: *this is too good to be true*, *I don't know what I did to deserve this*, or *this will never last*. You will also tolerate disrespect a lot more if you have low self-worth, often times you won't even recognise disrespect because your inner dialogue aligns with how others are treating you. If someone treats you in a way that is not respectful and you get an icky feeling in your stomach, it can be easy to brush it off because you don't really know what to do beyond the feeling itself— you don't know what it means to be treated differently or you don't believe that you deserve better. Things like this can be why there is often some type of turmoil in relationships when we start to heal and raise our vibrations. The other people involved in our lives are used to us acting and being a certain way. When we start to change ourselves and create boundaries then it shifts the energy and they often aren't sure what this means at first. They can make up stories in their minds to try and make sense of the energy they are feeling and sometimes react negatively. We can hear statements like "you've changed" but in a bitter, fearful, or angry tone because that person feels uncomfortable at first with this shift and uncomfortable with how it is forcing them to show up.

I used to hear the "you've changed" statement from my husband and it made me feel like I was doing something bad or wrong; this stemmed from a fear that he would not love me anymore if I changed. Once I was able to look at the fear itself and no longer needed to be attached to the story, I found myself standing securely in how I was transforming. I felt proud of myself when he'd say "you've changed" and I let him own his own fears behind the statement.

You can use your reactions to situations as your guides to healing. When someone says or does something and it triggers feelings of fear then you have an opportunity to explore it, heal, and move into a more loving space. Accepting yourself and your reaction is a good first step because it allows you to stand in the awareness of what it is teaching you instead of defaulting to self-criticism.

Acceptance and love for yourself will improve all areas of your relationships. You will no longer look for validation from others or feel that you need to be who you think they want you to be in order to earn their love. You will start to create a trust in yourself by showing up in a way that feels good to your heart rather than showing up in a way you perceive the world wants you to be.

Let's start to explore your soul on a deeper level and discover what nurturing a relationship with yourself looks like. Let's also explore where you can begin healing based on how you currently view yourself in relationships.

If I take away all limitations and stories of current or past relationships, what would my ideal spousal relationship look like? Consider this person's career, hobbies, values, how they treat you, common interests, spiritual/religious beliefs, how often you would spend time together, and so on.

Do I believe I deserve to have this type of ideal relationship with a significant other? Why or why not?

Where do I feel these beliefs come from?

What can I do to help myself stand more in the belief that I deserve to have this ideal relationship?

Who are the five people I spend the most time with?

_____

_____

_____

_____

How do I feel after I spend time with each of these people?

_____

_____

_____

_____

_____

_____

What do I value in each of these people?

_____

_____

_____

_____

_____

_____

How do each of these people inspire me?

_____

_____

_____

_____

_____

_____

_____

_____

_____

_____

Do I feel motivated to show each of these people love? If so, how do I show my love? If not, why do I think I lack the motivation?

_____

_____

_____

_____

_____

_____

Do I wish each of these people showed love differently? In what ways would I like them to showcase their love? Why is this important to me?

_____

_____

_____

_____

_____

_____

_____

How can I give myself more of the love that I wish they would show me?

_____

_____

_____

_____

_____

Is there anyone on this list of five people that I do not wish to continue a relationship with? Why?

_____

_____

_____

Is there anyone else in my life that I do not wish to currently continue a relationship with? Why?

_____

_____

_____

How can I expand my awareness of this person and the role they play in my life? What lessons do I believe this person brought me?

_____

_____

_____

_____

_____

Do I feel (at this time) that I can stand in a place of acceptance for this person and the relationship? Why or why not?

_____

_____

_____

_____

_____

_____

If I want to end the relationship, what fears do I have around doing this? Where do these fears come from?

_____

_____

_____

_____

Do I believe that people will love me if I am completely myself around them? Why or why not?

_____

_____

_____

_____

Do I believe that I am capable of hurting other people and that I am responsible for how they feel? Why or why not? Where do I feel this belief comes from?

_____

_____

_____

_____

_____

Do I have a fear of being alone? If yes, what about being alone am I afraid of?

_____

_____

_____

_____

_____

_____

_____

Do I believe I deserve to be loved by others? Why or why not?

_____

_____

_____

_____

Do I believe I deserve to be cared for by others? Why or why not?

_____

_____

_____

_____

Do I feel angry when those closest to me do not acknowledge when I am upset? Why or why not?

_____

_____

_____

_____

What do I feel like I am looking for from them in those moments? How can I give this to myself?

_____

_____

_____

_____

How do I feel when those closest to me do not acknowledge the things I am excited about or do not feel as excited about them as I do? Why do I feel this way?

_____

_____

_____

_____

When making decisions for myself, do I feel that I need others to agree with me in order to validate that it is the right thing to do? Why or why not?

_____

_____

_____

_____

What can I do to trust myself more to make the right decisions for my life without needing the opinions of others?

_____

_____

_____

_____

Are there any other relationships I currently have that I would like to nurture more than I have been? How would I like to do this?

_____

_____

_____

_____

_____

Do I believe that everyone comes into my life for a reason? Why or why not?

_____

_____

_____

_____

Do I believe that when people leave my life it is for a reason? Why or why not?

_____

_____

_____

_____

Are there any past relationships that have ended that I still feel hurt from? If so, what feelings do I have about them and the relationships?

_____

_____

_____

_____

How do I want to feel about my past relationships? What can I do to help me feel this way?

_____

_____

_____

_____

_____

Is there a person that I interact with that makes me feel irritated or drained? What kinds of personality traits do they have that irritate me?

_____

_____

_____

_____

How can I be more accepting of this person?

_____

_____

_____

_____

What kind of friend do I want to be? Why do I want to show up this way?

_____

_____

_____

_____

_____

What kind of daughter/son do I want to be? Why?

_____

_____

_____

_____

_____

_____

What kind of partner do I want to be? Why?

_____

_____

_____

_____

_____

_____

If I have or want children, what kind of parent do I want to be? Why?

_____

_____

_____

_____

_____

_____

_____

_____

If I have siblings, what kind of sister/brother do I want to be? Why?

_____

_____

_____

_____

_____

_____

Is there anything on these lists of what kind of person I want to be that I felt I wrote in order to earn acceptance in my relationships? If so, what were they?

_____

_____

_____

_____

Do I feel the people in each of my relationships will still love me if I don't show up the way I said I want to? Why or why not?

_____

_____

_____

_____

_____

Do I feel that I tolerate disrespect from family simply because of the title of the relationship? Why or why not?

_____

_____

_____

_____

_____

How would I like to show up differently in my relationships if I currently tolerate disrespect?

_____

_____

_____

When was a time I felt vibrant and alive in a relationship? What do I think contributed to feeling this way?

_____

_____

_____

_____

_____

How do I love to be loved?

_____

_____

_____

_____

_____

_____

_____

_____

_____

How can I show myself more love in these ways?

_____

_____

_____

_____

_____

Affirmations

I deserve to be loved.

My life is filled with healthy relationships.

I am responsible for how I feel.

I am willing to be loved.

My heart is safe.

I trust myself.

I am accepting of myself and others.

I am love.

Books

The Awakened Family by Shafali Tsabary, Ph.D.

The Five Love Languages by Gary Chapman

Everybody, Always: Love in a World Full of Setbacks and Difficult People by Bob Goff (Christianity)

Big Love: The Power of Living with a Wide-Open Heart

by Scott Stable

Love Yourself Like Your Life Depends on It by Kamal Ravikant

How to Love Yourself (and Sometimes Other People): Spiritual Advice for Modern Relationships by Meggan Watterson and Londro Rinzler

Gratitude

Today I am grateful for:

_____

_____

_____

_____

_____

_____

_____

Moments of Joy

Today's moments of joy:

_____

_____

_____

_____

_____

_____

_____

_____

Forgiveness

Forgiveness is such a pivotal aspect of living a soulful life. The most magical and divine love I have ever felt stem from moments of massive forgiveness, and these experiences led to some of my biggest transformations. Sometimes our spirits can't cope with looking at all of the hurt at once, so forgiveness tends to show up in layers that we continuously evolve through. Piece by piece, we forgive a little at a time.

Forgiveness gives you freedom from the prison of pain and hurt. It is liberating! The freedom in forgiveness begins with understanding your freedom of choice. You do not have to forgive; rather, you get to decide if you *want* to forgive. You can choose to look at what the person and experiences taught you, and focus on being grateful for the lessons, instead of allowing the hurt to take over every part of your life. I understand that this is not always as easy as just saying it. People can get quite frustrated on this topic because they hear the word forgiveness and then spin around in guilt and frustration for still feeling pain and not being able to let it go. I believe it is more important for us to focus on creating an environment where forgiveness thrives. This involves looking at every area of the self and your life journey, which you are doing now by working through this guide.

Forgiveness does not excuse the behaviour, but it sure as hell can feel like it! We can fight so hard to justify our pain to the point that it can become our identity; we can forget who we are outside of the pain because it is always in the forefront of our minds, influencing every thought and feeling we have.

You can get caught in these positions without really knowing how to stop this cycle of pain because you aren't really sure how you got stuck there in the first place. Often it is such a gradual process that it happens without us being aware of it until we are in really deep. Sometimes people become aware of the depth of their pain and what it has created in their life and they don't want to let go because of the fear of the unknown. They have been receiving some level of sympathy for what they experienced for such a long time that they can find it difficult to believe they will receive any kind of love and affection without it.

Justifying your pain also applies when you are looking at forgiving yourself for things you have done that hurt yourself or other people. It is easier to make yourself believe that you deserve to feel the pain for what you did than it is to forgive yourself and use the experience to move forward a better person. Your guilt turns into shame and you go from believing that what you did is bad, to *I am a bad person.* You justify your pain and stay stuck in your own prison while holding the key in your hand.

My husband gave me the most eye opening insight into this pattern. A few years after the affair in our marriage, there were some couples we knew who were going through similar situations to what we went through. The difference was that some of the spouses continued on with their painful patterns; they didn't see the depth of hurt they were causing to themselves and their families. I asked my husband why he thought they were doing that. What was it that made him come home, face all of the hurt, and want to rebuild his life, but they didn't? You could feel the emotions take over him and he said, "Amanda, sometimes it is easier to just be the asshole. You have already caused so much pain to yourself and everyone you love, so it is just easier to be that person people now expect you to be than it is to face everyone and face yourself. You get caught up in this belief that no one will ever see you any differently now and you don't know how to get out, so it is easier to just be the asshole."

We may not be perfect people, but we are all beautiful souls created from the same source. Forgiveness gives you the freedom to choose your soul above anything else. Learning who you are outside of your pain and loving who that person is helps you to move beyond the identity created from your pain. As you cultivate an environment where forgiveness thrives, you will slowly start to see that you are worthy of the freedom forgiveness brings.

Forgiving people who are sorry for their actions is very different than forgiving people who are still actively trying to hurt you and are not sorry. There is a divine and unconditional love that comes with accepting people who hurt you and do not see an issue with their actions. Forgiving them is more about trusting the flow of life and thanking their soul for showing up right on time to help you grow. It is about focusing on the energy you are creating in your world. It does not excuse their behaviour, but it does give you your power back.

When people experience some level of trauma in their life their nervous system kicks into over drive and they go into fight or flight mode. Our bodies can actually become addicted to being in this heightened state as our thoughts replay the painful experience over and over again and our body responds accordingly. Over time our body finds it difficult to relax and our thoughts begin to respond to the physical stress we feel. In other words, they start to become familiar with each other and our body becomes addicted to being stressed—even while we are sleeping, we are not able to get a full REM (rapid eye movement) sleep. When we start to think about the painful memories, the thoughts easily spin out of control and we don't notice our body has kicked into high gear.

Healing starts with the awareness of your thoughts, their patterns, and your triggers. After you learn to become more aware of them, you can start to choose thoughts that align more with how you want to feel. As you go through this process, you will notice moments where you defend or justify the old thought patterns. Our ego likes to keep us safe, it likes the comfort of what is familiar, so it will make you believe it is better to hold onto the painful thoughts than to release them. Forgiveness is about listening more to your heart. We are not meant to stay angry and resentful in our life. Our natural state is love, and forgiveness brings us to the most divine love there is!

If you are still struggling with choosing thoughts that align with how you want to feel, try to take the significance out of the pain attached to the old thought and put it into the lessons the experience taught you. If you do not know what those lessons are, you might still be avoiding the pain itself. Sit quietly and take a few deep breaths and set the intention that you are going to welcome the pain into your awareness. Remember that you are not the pain itself; you are simply a soul experiencing it. The pain does not control you. Focus on your heart space opening up, be willing to feel what it needs to feel, and then embrace the awareness of yourself that comes as a result. This does not mean you need to relive the experience, it just means you won't fight away or push down the emotions trying to release from your body.

As you start to choose thoughts that align more with moving beyond your pain and into how you want to feel, you will slowly start to see a different picture of your life. You will start to believe the new thoughts and truly feel you deserve better for yourself.

Some people feel stuck with forgiving because they feel fear around trusting people or a specific person again. The truth is, trust never is and never was about the other person. It is about the trust you have for yourself. We all have the capacity to do the same things that others have done to us. I think everyone has experienced a gut feeling about something that they didn't listen to but, as you heal and start to live a more soulful life, you will develop a stronger trust in yourself. You will begin to do what is right for you no matter what happens in your life. No longer will you ignore your intuition; instead, you will listen to it and allow it to guide you.

We never know how we are going to respond to something until we are living it, and if we go on expecting that bad things will happen, then they always will. If you are attempting to heal a relationship, then it does not take away the other person's responsibility of owning their actions and supporting you in feeling secure in the relationship. Your job is to be honest with yourself and the other person—preferably with a sense of compassion. Everything changes and everyone changes. Giving and receiving forgiveness is a step towards peace.

Let's begin to explore where forgiveness is needed in your life and how to develop a deeper trust in yourself.

When I think of forgiveness, what other thoughts and feelings initially come with it?

_____

_____

_____

_____

_____

_____

When are times in my life where I felt deeply hurt by someone else?

_____

_____

_____

_____

_____

_____

What feelings come up when I think of this person or people and the memories?

_____

_____

_____

_____

_____

_____

If I imagine each person individually, can I freely send them love, or do I feel hesitation and resistance?

_____

_____

_____

_____

_____

Do I feel guilt or frustration with myself if I don't want to forgive? Why?

_____

_____

_____

_____

_____

Is there a time in my life where someone else was hurt because of something I did? If yes, what did I do?

_____

_____

_____

_____

_____

What thoughts do I have about myself when I think about my actions and how people were hurt by them?

_____

_____

_____

_____

_____

Do I want to continue believing these thoughts about myself? Why or why not?

_____

_____

_____

_____

_____

What thoughts and feelings do I have when I know that someone has lied to me?

_____

_____

_____

_____

Do I feel that forgiveness justifies the behaviour of the other person? Why or why not?

_____

_____

_____

_____

_____

When I think of someone who has hurt me and I think about forgiving them, does the forgiveness come from a place of love or from a place of trying to push the pain away? Why?

_____

_____

_____

_____

_____

If there is anyone that I still hold anger and resentment towards, can I be open to the idea of forgiving them? Why or why not?

_____

_____

_____

_____

Do I feel ready to forgive them now?

_____

_____

If yes, what does my life look like from a place of total forgiveness? If no, what can I do to become ready to forgive?

_____

_____

_____

_____

_____

_____

_____

When I think of someone I have not yet fully forgiven, what do I feel I need in order to take my power back?

_____

_____

_____

_____

_____

Is there something I am afraid of knowing or losing if I fully forgive?

_____

_____

_____

_____

Am I willing to open my heart and release the emotions attached to the person and painful experience? Why? What would happen if I didn't?

_____

_____

_____

_____

How can I support myself through this process of awareness and release?

_____

_____

_____

_____

In my own words, what does it mean to me to choose my soul? What does this feel like?

_____

_____

_____

_____

What is something I can do every day to help me create an environment where I am better able to forgive?

_____

_____

_____

_____

When looking at situations where I was hurt, can I be open to the idea of accepting that I cannot change what has happened? Why or why not?

_____

_____

_____

_____

Is there a time I remember having a gut feeling about something but I did not follow the feeling? If yes, what was it? What happened as a result?

_____

_____

_____

_____

Do I feel frustration or anger at myself for not listening to my intuition in that moment?

_____

_____

Can I accept that I did the best I could in that moment? Why or why not?

_____

_____

_____

_____

_____

Can I love who I was in that moment? Why or why not?

_____

_____

_____

_____

Can I be willing to accept that the people whose actions I was hurt by were doing the best they could in that moment? Why or why not?

_____

_____

_____

_____

_____

When I think of a situation where I felt pain or trauma, what lessons do I feel I took away from the experience?

_____

_____

_____

_____

_____

_____

_____

Do I feel these lessons support me in moving towards more divine love and awareness? Why or why not?

_____

_____

_____

What can I do every day to help me focus on the significance of the lessons these painful experiences brought me?

_____

_____

_____

How can I also support my body in physically healing as I heal emotionally?

_____

_____

_____

When I think or talk about the painful experience, how do I tell the story?

_____

_____

_____

_____

How can I tell the story differently so that it focuses on the beautiful lessons I took away from the experience?

Affirmations

I accept the past and embrace the future.

It is safe to forgive.

I love who I am becoming.

I am willing to forgive.

I embrace the love in my life.

My intuition is clear and strong.

I live in the present.

I take responsibility for the energy I create in my life.

Book Recommendations

A Return To Love by Marianne Williamson

Gratitude

Today I am grateful for:

_____

_____

_____

_____

_____

_____

_____

Moments of Joy

Today's moments of joy:

_____

_____

_____

_____

_____

_____

_____

_____

Your Emotional Self

Life can feel like a rollercoaster sometimes—an overwhelming one! Our emotions play a big part in how we experience life and it is important to make friends with them so that we can understand them better. In this section we are going to explore what it means for you to truly honour your emotions, how to make sense of them, and why this is important.

Many people grow up with the belief that some emotions are bad and some are good. Yes, some emotions don't feel as good as others, but they are all part of the flow of life and each one serves us in its own way. People can create stories around certain emotions often as a result of a negative response from someone else. For example, if you were sad and crying but someone did not feel your reason for being sad was justified, then you might feel wrong for expressing that emotion or feeling it at all. So instead of seeing how the other person was simply triggered from you expressing your emotion, you took it personally and decided that crying without a justified reason (based on someone else's opinion) was no longer acceptable. In order to avoid judgement going forward, you continued on with life and pushed the sadness down if it ever got to the point of tears. After doing this for a period of time people can forget the originating factor that created this feeling and just accept it as their truth.

Common belief structures such as *boys don't cry, anger is not healthy, spiritual people are supposed to be calm and collected, and girls are too much if they cry*, can start to imprint our beliefs from very young ages. Even if the comments and judgements are not directed at you specifically, it can be easy to attach to them in order to avoid judgement and pain. When we struggle with low self-worth these types of patterns can take over without us even being aware of it. Children are very impressionable when they are young as they are trying to understand life and where they fit in, while receiving almost constant direction from others. This can be such a confusing time and, as adults, we have the opportunities to work through any perceived limitations we may have attached to, and use them as part of the foundation to living authentically now.

It is important that you first get clear on the stories you tell yourself in regards to experiencing and expressing your emotions. Once you have a deeper awareness to what these stories are you have the power to heal and change them... if you want to. You can start to build a deeper trust and connection to your soul by honouring each emotion that presents itself.

The practice of honouring your emotions is: welcoming them in, being aware of your reactions, allowing the emotions to be present with you for as long as they are needed, accepting yourself as the person who is experiencing the emotion at that moment, and—when you feel the emotions leaving on their own—asking yourself what you need to help you move forward.

Emotions are energy and when you supress them they do not just disappear; instead, they sit in your body and fester. The buildup over time can greatly affect your physical health and your overall mental wellbeing, including contributing to anxiety and depression. Louise Hay's book *You Can Heal Your Life* is a great guide to showing you which emotions are linked to physical illnesses and injuries. The body and mind have a very powerful connection!

Many people with anxiety and depression can feel a great amount of fear when it comes to honouring their emotions. The thought of doing this can trigger fears of losing control and not knowing how to get out of the spiral. There is no doubt this can be scary at first! It is important to remember you are a soul experiencing a human life. If you can step back and witness the emotions as something that is part of the human experience, you can see that they can't control you. You can see your soul as being bigger than the emotion itself. It can be very beneficial to have help with this in the beginning by having someone talk you through the process so that you feel a little safer as you step into your power.

Acceptance of yourself and the situation is a pivotal moment in the honouring process. Accepting that you are the person feeling angry and reacting in the moment, but not judging yourself for it, is very empowering. It takes you from a state of confusion and victimization to being a soulful human who is ready to move forward by saying, "Ok! This is how I'm feeling right now." This step requires your willingness to release expectations of yourself and others.

This requires taking full ownership of what you are feeling and understanding how you need to move through the feeling. Sometimes the people you share your life with will know how to support you through this and sometimes they won't. Sometimes they will be directly affected by your reactions and they will need the freedom to have their own responses. This is about you taking a step backward and inward to honour yourself and then stepping forward again with clarity on the situation to say to anyone else involved, "Ok... here is what I learned through this experience."

It is ok to apologize if your reactions hurt someone but you do not need to justify them. Out of love for the other person and love for yourself, you can explain how you felt and maybe why you reacted the way you did; however, justifying and explaining carry a different energy. Justifying carries the energy of needing validation that who you are is good based on the perspective of someone else. Explaining carries the energy of love and respect for the other people involved but you still stand in your power with love for yourself as well.

Having tools in place to help you through the process of honouring your emotions can be very helpful. Meditation is an amazing practice to help you be present and gain clarity to what it is you need in the moment. Journaling through the beginning stages of feeling an overwhelm of emotions can be beneficial if you take the time to sit and dump all of your thoughts onto paper. This helps you sift through them instead of spinning the same thoughts over and over again. The emotion or feeling is what triggers the thoughts, then the thoughts trigger more emotions, and before we know it, we feel overwhelmed when this cycle continues. Journaling to get to the core feelings will give you more clarity, help you feel lighter, and you might not need to sit in the emotions as long.

Looking at your emotions and responses to find out what is triggering them is the step that helps you move forward. What fears are being brought up? Getting clear on the fear will help you realign with the truth. For example, if your spouse asks why you didn't do the laundry and you instantly feel anger towards him for not appreciating all the work you do or for not noticing how busy you are, then you might react by yelling at him to do it himself or by giving him the silent treatment while you feel furious inside. By accepting how you are feeling you could sit down and write out all the thoughts you were having and acknowledge how upset you are with him. When you are done you could ask yourself, "Why did that bother me so much?" Maybe his question triggered the deeper fear and belief that you are not good enough or that you always have to be working to earn his love and approval.

Next, ask yourself, "When is another time in my life that I felt like I had to earn people's love or that I felt like what I did was not good enough?" When you get to the core emotion you can see what really fueled your thoughts and reaction. You can then reflect upon what you need in that moment to love and accept yourself, and to remind yourself that what you do is enough. Even if you do nothing, you are still enough and you still deserve to be loved. This is connecting to your truth! This is reconnecting to your soul! The truth is: you are already enough because you are created from a divine source, which means you are divine, and you *are* love! Revisit the situation from this space of love and tell your partner how his question made you feel and why it made you feel that way. Consider how you could ask for help and share what would make you feel supported.

I found that my reactions to situations happened less and less as I practiced this process. The more I deepened my awareness of what was at the root of my reactions and connected to my truth, the more I felt calm and confident in myself. I no longer needed to give myself a voice or react from a space of defensiveness; instead, I began honouring my emotions from a space of love and understanding. This took practice! I had to go through the (e)motions so many times to better understand myself and heal so that I could be more accepting of my emotions and the emotions of others. I noticed this reflected a lot in my parenting as well. Now when my boys feel frustrated and get angry I don't tell them not to react or feel that way. If they are really losing their cool I send them to their rooms and let them work it out and calm down. When they are done I ask if they are ready to talk about it with me. We even have times where we just scream in the car if one of us is upset. It starts out as needing to let go and release, and then turns into us laughing because we feel better. Since the boys are getting older, we are going to invest in a punching bag so that they have a safe space to let out their anger. The point is, everybody's feelings matter regardless of age, race, gender, or status. What is important is that we release them in an appropriate way.

Another aspect of understanding your emotional self is understanding grief. When you lose someone you love you go through a whirlwind of emotions that can hit you at the most unexpected times. Once the dust settles, and you try to regain some sense of normalcy in your life, you can go through an influx of guilt, anger, sadness, frustration, and more unwanted feelings. You can go from being happy one minute to crying the next; you can experience happiness and grief simultaneously—neither is wrong. Even if you have the most unshakable trust and faith in the process of life, you can still feel grief and sadness when you lose someone you love. Try not to get caught up in what grief is supposed to look like. Focus more on what it looks like for you because everyone moves through it differently. Everyone needs different things at different times. Grieving doesn't actually end, it just evolves.

Let's take some time now to have a better understanding of your emotional self.

What emotions do I struggle to feel and/or express?

_____

_____

_____

_____

When I think of expressing those emotions what fears come up?

_____

_____

_____

_____

_____

Which fear would I like to focus on first so as to stand more in my truth? Why do I choose this fear over the other ones?

_____

_____

_____

_____

_____

Are there any fears on that list that I feel myself wanting to stay attached to? Why or why not?

_____

_____

_____

_____

Are there any statements or judgements about expressing emotions that I remember people saying when I was young?

_____

_____

_____

_____

_____

Do I feel those statements affect me now? If yes, how? If no, why not?

_____

_____

_____

_____

_____

Do I feel I react to situations or people more than I would like to? If yes, why do I feel like I react so easily?

_____

_____

_____

_____

_____

What do I need to support myself better in moving through all of my emotions?

_____

_____

_____

_____

_____

When was a time in my life (or a relationship) where I felt heard and understood?

_____

_____

_____

_____

Who is someone in my life now that I can trust to listen to me when I am feeling an overwhelm of emotions? Why do I trust them?

_____

_____

_____

_____

When I am feeling angry, what is a way I can express or release that anger freely without taking it out on anyone directly?

_____

_____

_____

Do I find myself wishing people understood how I was feeling without needing to tell them? If yes, why?

_____

_____

_____

_____

Do I feel like I am a burden to others if I cry in front of them and make them uncomfortable? If yes, why?

_____

_____

_____

_____

_____

_____

Do I feel better afterwards if I let myself have a good cry when I am sad, or punch a pillow when I am angry?

_____

_____

In my own words, why do I feel it is important to honour all of my emotions?

_____

_____

_____

_____

_____

_____

Do I believe that I am a soul experiencing human emotions, If yes, why? If no, what do I believe about the emotions I experience?

_____

_____

_____

_____

_____

_____

_____

Do my beliefs feel good and do they support me in what kind of person I want to be? Why or Why not?

_____

_____

_____

_____

Affirmations

It is safe for me to express my emotions.

I allow my authentic self to be expressed.

I am solely responsible for how I feel.

I am open to the healing that my emotions and awareness bring me.

I am worthy of affection and love.

Book Recommendations

Anatomy of The Spirit by Caroline Myss

Transforming Depression by Doc Childre and Deborah Rozman

Option B: Facing Adversity, Building Resilience, and Finding Joy by Sheryl Sandberg and Adam M. Grant

Insight: Why We're Not as Self-Aware as We Think, and How Seeing Ourselves Clearly Helps Us Succeed at Work and in Life by Tasha Eurich

Healing Trauma by Peter A. Levine

When the Body Says No: The Cost of Hidden Stress

by Gabor Mate

Gratitude

Today I am grateful for:

_____

_____

_____

_____

_____

_____

_____

_____

Moments of Joy

Today's moments of joy:

_____

_____

_____

_____

_____

_____

_____

_____

_____

Your Physical Self

Fully embracing and loving the body you are in is another powerful step along your path to healing. So often we blindly criticise our body and physical appearance that we don't see how this criticism limits us from stepping into our full potential.

Living a more soulful life this means embracing the beauty that is our physical self. If our soul is created from divine source energy, then it cannot be separate from it. Source is perfect; therefore, your soul is perfect as well. While your soul was creating a life that would help it learn and evolve it decided that this body, which you currently reside, would be perfect in helping it to achieve all of those things. Denying this body is denying your truth!

You can spend so much of your time criticising your body or wishing it was different that, after a while, you don't even hear what you are saying. You become so numb to the hate, and it is difficult to change something you don't really see. I did not realize how much time I spent wishing my body was different in some way until I made a point of actively paying attention to my thoughts every time I looked in the mirror. I started writing those thoughts down and, as I read them over, I imagined my inner child and pictured her sweet little face. When I heard those words being spoken to her, it broke my heart. She was none of those things.

I remember a meditation where I connected to myself as a little girl. I asked her what she needed from me. I was not expecting her response but she said, "I need you to love your curly hair because when you don't you make me feel ugly." This hit me so hard. I did not see how much I was denying a piece of me that was a natural part of my being. Plus, it made my heart sad at the thought of calling her ugly while seeing her standing there with her cute overalls and bouncy golden brown curls.

My hair can be wild when it is curly and there is no way of knowing if it is going to be a good curly hair day or a wickedly bad one, so most times it is easier for me to straighten it and have more *control*. This is where I started being aware of the thoughts I had about my physical appearance. Every time I went to wash my hair for a straight hair day (because you need to wash your hair differently when it is curly) I would ask myself, *Why*? *Why am I doing this?* "Because no one thinks you are pretty with this wild hair, Amanda." "Because I will have to spend extra time putting makeup on if my hair is curly so that I don't look like a man." "Because if I let my hair go naturally then the top half might get stringy and that doesn't look good." This list went on and on.

I had to breathe and practice speaking kindly to myself about my hair. It felt uncomfortable at first because I had never really done that before. I found myself looking to my husband quite often to give me some sort of validation that he still thought I was pretty if my hair was curly that day. Even if he said he did, I would find some reason for his compliment to not be enough. I didn't want to give up because I knew I was going against many years of programing on this one. I realized that I couldn't expect myself to feel differently right away. To this day, I still work on loving my hair and every other part of my appearance. It feels a little more freeing each time I do.

Nourishing your physical self requires many layers and is a journey like everything else in this life. Sometimes your negative talk around your physical self can still be masked even if you exercise regularly and eat a strict healthy diet. If you spend your entire exercise routine focusing on how you wish your body was different instead of thanking it for being healthy and strong, then you are not embracing and loving your body. If you eat healthy from a space of fear then you are only putting the energy of fear into your body. It is important to find the balance of love and acceptance of your body as it is now, while still making sure you take care of it and nurture it in the way it is asking you to.

Meditation is a great way to connect with your body and ask what it needs. You will need to practice relaxing into your breath and asking your body, "What do you need from me to feel loved and nourished?" Then feel yourself mentally and physically sinking back into your seat which helps put you into receiving mode for the messages. Allow the messages to come without judgement and to show up in whatever way they need to. For example, the last time I did this meditation my body showed me three main things it needed but each of the messages came forward in a different way.

The first message presented itself as a feeling where I became very thirsty in an instant. My body felt like a dry desert and I had a knowing that this meant I needed to drink more water. The second message came forward as a color. I saw a flash of red in my mind and the thought of spices arose. So when I thought of adding more red spices to my diet I felt a lightness and sort of a release which meant that this was the message my body wanted to tell me. I could also feel the connection of the color red to my root chakra and my body craving that grounded acceptance of myself and feelings of security. The last message came to me as an overwhelming feeling of love. I had my hands on my stomach to help focus on my breathing and the feeling of my body rising and falling with each breath. I felt a shift of focus go to my body and the loving feeling of it under my hands. It reminded me of holding a baby and gently rubbing its back to comfort it. I remember asking myself, "How often do I love my body that way?" My body was asking me to love it and hold it this way, especially on my stomach where it once was flat and now has a pouch, a stretched out belly button, and scars from carrying my boys.

Now at least once a day I will put my hands on my stomach and feel that same kind of love for my body that you would give to your child: an unconditional and grateful love!

Our bodies are so intelligent and have this incredible ability to tell us what they need. Illness can be another way your body is trying to tell you what you need on a physical and emotional level. Sometimes getting the flu at the most inconvenient time is your body trying to tell you to slow down and remind you that you do not need to try so hard in life. A sore throat can be sign that you are not speaking your truth and it is asking you to find your voice. I had to fight a lot of my old stories to stop eating meat and listen to my body when it felt sick and exhausted every time I ate it. I felt so much lighter once I did and I do not guilt myself or feel fear if my body is craving a little piece of chicken and I eat it!

Noticing how you judge others and their physical appearance can be a good indicator of where you stand with your own insecurities about your body. This can be anything from the shape of their body, to the color of their hair, or how many tattoos they have. Realizing that we all just *human* a little differently and standing in a space of love will help us to see our judgements of others as a way to deepen our awareness of our own fears. It will also show us where we can heal. You can practice receiving more love from yourself by actually sending love to other people. If you see someone who you would perceive as overweight and catch yourself judging them, then you can switch your thoughts to thinking kindly of them and seeing their beautiful soul above anything else. Remember we are all connected, so loving them is loving yourself.

Finding ways to support yourself in cultivating new and loving thoughts about your body is important. Putting loving messages up throughout your house that remind you to be kind to your body can help start to shift the way you feel about yourself. Every time someone gives you a compliment practice simply receiving it instead of pushing it away or needing to reciprocate it immediately. You do not need a grand response, a simple thank you is enough. Over time this will support you in truly believing that you deserve love and affection and are loved just the way you are.

Notice how the people around you judge others or how they speak about their own bodies. It can be easy to take these thoughts on as your own truth if you are not being aware of your own dialogue as well. If their words match what you already believe to be true then they are just validation and you can become numb to them. If what they are saying does not align with how you want to feel about yourself, you can simply shift your focus to your own lane and not allow yourself to attach to what they are saying. In these moments I like to take a second to remind myself who I am and that I love my body just as it is. After a while I even built up the courage to start complimenting people when they would judge themselves in some way. Or, if they were judging someone else, I would try and say something kind about that person and use words of support for them to just be who they are. I would try and feed any negativity with love!

The practice of loving your body more is going to take time and it will evolve. Try different things as you feel yourself growing and shifting into a greater love. Just like anything else, it is most important to be present with the process and know that you will get there. I like to look at it as coming home to myself, because when I was born I already loved myself completely and had complete trust in what I was here to do... I just forgot for a little while. I work every day to come home to that truth of my soul. This takes patience, vulnerability, trust, and acceptance to create the kind of love you are striving for.

Let's dive into discovering how you can cultivate that deep unconditional love for your physical self.

If I stand in the mirror and look at my body, which parts do I wish were different? Why do I wish each part was different?

_____

_____

_____

_____

_____

What do I believe it means to be physically healthy?

_____

_____

_____

Where does this belief come from?

_____

_____

_____

Does this belief support fully loving my body?

_____

_____

Do I believe I can love my body as it is now and still strive to nurture it by eating healthier and exercising?

_____

_____

What can I do every day to help me focus on loving my body more, as it is now?

_____

_____

_____

_____

What habits do I currently have that do not feel good to my body when considering eating, smoking, alcohol, drugs, exercise, thoughts/beliefs, hygiene, and sleep?

_____

_____

_____

_____

How do each of these habits affect me physically, mentally, and emotionally?

_____

_____

_____

_____

_____

_____

_____

_____

_____

What thoughts come up when I feel like justifying and continuing these habits?

_____

_____

_____

_____

What new habits have I had a curiosity for or have been coming to my mind a lot lately? For example, trying a new yoga or kick boxing class, or adding/eliminating something from my diet.

_____

_____

_____

When I think of implementing these new habits, what excuses come up that make me believe it would be too difficult?

_____

_____

_____

Why do I want to love my body more?

_____

_____

_____

What are some phrases I can use to speak kindly to my body?

_____

_____

_____

_____

_____

_____

Do I find it difficult to speak kindly to the parts of my body that I wish were different? Why or why not?

_____

_____

_____

_____

Did my parents speak about their physical appearance in front of me when I was young? What do I remember about what they said or how they felt about themselves?

_____

_____

_____

_____

Do I feel pressured by society to look a certain way? Why or why not?

_____

_____

_____

_____

_____

How can I be more mindful about giving people compliments?

_____

_____

_____

_____

_____

What kinds of compliments would I like to give to people more?

_____

_____

_____

_____

Do I feel nervous about complimenting people after they have put themselves down? Why or why not?

_____

_____

_____

_____

Do I give excuses or shut down compliments when people give them to me?

_____

_____

Do I believe I deserve to be complimented? Why or why not?

_____

_____

_____

_____

_____

Are there things I find unattractive about other people? (Body types, tattoos, hair color/style, piercings, and clothing styles, for example.)

_____

_____

_____

_____

What judging thoughts do I have about people who have features that I find unattractive? What beliefs do I have about these people?

_____

_____

_____

_____

_____

Where can I see my own fears in the judgements I have of others based on their appearance?

_____

_____

_____

_____

Can I be open to being more accepting of others based on their appearance? Why or why not?

_____

_____

_____

_____

Try the meditation I spoke about earlier where you connect to your body and ask what it needs to feel loved and nourished. Write what messages came forward for you in this meditation.

_____

_____

_____

_____

_____

_____

How can I implement the messages my body brought forward during my meditation?

_____

_____

_____

_____

How has my body supported me and how can I thank it every day for doing those things?

_____

_____

_____

_____

_____

Are there any foods I currently eat that make my body feel heavy or sluggish?

_____

_____

_____

_____

_____

What stories do I have around these foods and why do I keep eating them?

_____

_____

_____

_____

Would I like to eliminate those foods at this time? Why or why not?

_____

_____

_____

_____

How can I support myself in eliminating them?

_____

_____

_____

_____

_____

What ways do I look to others to validate my physical appearance?

_____

_____

_____

_____

Do I feel fulfilled and satisfied when they validate me in these ways?

_____

_____

How can I give myself more of this validation?

_____

_____

_____

_____

What compliments would I give to my younger self?

_____

_____

_____

_____

_____

_____

_____

Take the list you wrote about all the things you wish were different about your body and read it aloud to your younger self. Visualize her standing in front of you as you read it. How did this make you feel?

_____

_____

_____

_____

_____

_____

_____

_____

What does it mean to fully love my body and appearance? Why does this matter?

_____

_____

_____

_____

_____

_____

Do I feel I can be patient with myself through this process of loving my body more? Why or why not?

_____

_____

_____

_____

_____

_____

What reminders can I set in place to help remember the truths I have discovered in this journaling process?

_____

_____

_____

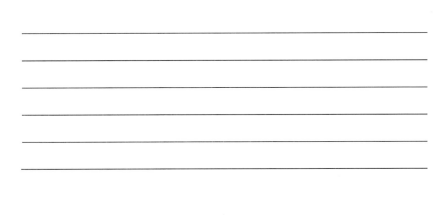

Affirmations

I honour my body's process. I honour my body.

I accept myself.

I am beautiful.

I am healthy.

I am radiant.

I see clearly what my body needs.

My body is a limitless reflection of my soul.

Book Recommendations

Medical Medium by Anthony William

Quantum Healing by Deepak Chopra

Gratitude

Today I am grateful for:

_____

_____

_____

_____

_____

_____

_____

_____

Moments of Joy

Today's moments of joy:

_____

_____

_____

_____

_____

_____

_____

_____

_____

Career

Throughout our lives our precious time is typically spent working more than it is spent doing anything else. It is incredibly important to discuss what a soulful life looks like in regards to our day-to-day jobs because we log so many hours making a living. Since this is such a vast topic, it required me to spend extra time journaling and meditating in order to get clear on the focus for this section. Everyone perceives work differently and knowing this caused me to be stuck in my head with what needed to be shared in this space. I had to sit in the love of spirit, play in that energy, and repeatedly revisit the *why* behind this guide.

When I got out of my head and into my heart I could feel and see how much my career matters to me. I don't feel like I am fully living if I am not doing the kind of work that I do. My work compliments me, enhances my life, and is a vessel for so many things that help me feel fulfilled.

As I wrote that truth in my journal it was as if spirit lit a huge lightbulb over my head and I felt a huge release of energy around me. I could see that it does not matter if you work 9-5 as a receptionist, get up at 4am to clock in at your local bakery, stay home to take care of your children, work countless hours managing a farm, or are an entrepreneur working multiple platforms. Living soulfully means that your work is a vessel to share your light with the world! When you love what you do and are excited to get up every day and work at your job, then you automatically raise your vibration and move into having more flow in your life. You will feel happier and lighter which means you are more likely to share that light with the people around you.

Sharing your light could mean anything—from being more patient with a co-worker who is still learning the new computer system, giving good customer service (because you want to and not because you are required to), finding inspiration with new project ideas, bringing a more positive outlook to difficult situations, and not feeling as easily affected by other co-workers or customers who are bringing a lower vibration of energy. The list could go on.

I think we all know what it feels like to meet someone who is happy to be at their job and they make us feel good just by being around them. This does not mean you need to show up to work every day bouncing with happiness if you have a bad day or you are dealing with other difficult transitions in your life. You are human. You will have down days; however, you will still feel a sense of peacefulness and contentment in your work and how it fits into your life on a whole.

Sometimes when we look at our working life we can be faced with limiting beliefs about what we *should* be doing or influenced by a multitude of socially acceptable rules. For example, a common belief would be that you are unreliable or don't know what you want in life if you change your job often. You are not living in a space of love for yourself if you believe that you need to stay at a job just to prove something to other people or make them more comfortable. All of my jobs have been incredible stepping stones to get me to where I am today. Each one supported me for who I was at that time in my life and taught me valuable lessons that I needed to better stand in the job I have now. At this point, I have no idea where this road will take me, but I can be present with what I am doing and creating in my life right now. I trust that each moment will continue to guide me.

But what about money? That's why most people work, right? Money can be a crippling factor when it comes to doing what you love. After all, we have bills to pay, food to put on the table, and trips to take. Your ego can easily make you believe that taking risks is not a good idea; it wants you to stay in the illusion of security. Quite often people tell themselves they have time and will eventually follow their passion in life, but this is usually a fear statement. The truth is that we don't always have time. Money is simply energy and it all depends on how you choose to align with it. You could have the *security* of the well-paying job and still manifest your furnace breaking down or getting a back injury if you are out of sync with your soul.

If you do not currently have a job and want one, then it would be wise to get clear on what brings you joy and how you love to spend your days. Asking the universe for help in bringing you the ideal job requires trust and a clearer vision of how you would feel doing that job. Then you can work on looking at any blocks you might have that are getting in your way of manifesting that job and cultivating the feelings you want from it.

Let's explore what your ideal job is and how to step into the joy of living that life, or how to nurture your current job if you are already doing what you love.

If there was no such thing as money, what would I do for work? What do I love to share with the world?

_____

_____

_____

_____

Why would I want to have this job? How do I feel it would enhance my life? How do I believe this job will make me feel if I had it?

_____

_____

_____

_____

_____

_____

Am I currently taking steps to move towards having this type of job?

_____

If yes, what are the steps I've already taken and what would be my next step?

_____

_____

_____

_____

If no, do I want to take steps towards having that job? Why or why not?

_____

_____

_____

_____

_____

Do I believe I deserve to have this type of job? Why or why not?

_____

_____

_____

_____

_____

What are my fears with having a job like this?

_____

_____

_____

_____

_____

Do any of the limiting beliefs that I wrote about in previous sections show up for me when I look at having my ideal job? If so, which ones?

_____

_____

_____

_____

How can I continue to support myself in moving beyond those limiting beliefs and making this dream job a reality?

_____

_____

_____

_____

When I am at my current job, do I wish I was doing something else? If so, what do I wish I was doing?

_____

_____

_____

_____

What do I love about my current job? Why do I love these aspects of it?

_____

_____

_____

_____

_____

What do I not love about my current job? Why do I not love these aspects of it?

_____

_____

_____

_____

_____

Do the things I do not love about my job feel like deal breakers for me? Why or why not?

_____

_____

_____

_____

_____

_____

How can I focus more on what I love about my current job?

_____

_____

_____

_____

How can I bring more love and positivity to my work?

_____

_____

_____

_____

_____

When I think of what kind of person I want to be, does my job support me in being that person?

_____

_____

If I stop loving my job, do I feel I can leave whenever I want? Why or why not?

_____

_____

_____

_____

Does my job allow me to nurture other areas of my life like my family and my health?

If no, what steps could I take to start creating space for this?

_____

_____

_____

_____

If yes, do I feel I want to nurture this balance more and what steps would I like to take to do this?

_____

_____

_____

_____

_____

Affirmations

I openly share my light with others.

I am deserving of happiness.

My heart is open to the beautiful possibilities of today.

I create joy everywhere I go.

Book Recommendations

Wishes Fulfilled by Wayne Dyer

QBQ! The Question Behind the Question: Practicing Personal Accountability in Work and in Life by John G. Miller and David L. Levin

Gratitude

Today I am grateful for:

_____

_____

_____

_____

_____

_____

_____

_____

Moments of Joy

Today's moments of joy:

_____

_____

_____

_____

_____

_____

_____

_____

_____

_____

_____

Your Journey Forward

My love, you have come so far! This guide has taken you through the main topics I discuss with my clients and the ideas we explore behind living a life of freedom and fulfillment. You should be so proud of yourself for stepping up and trying something new, for being present with yourself in these pages and discovering what healing looks like for you. This is no easy task but you showed up and you deserve to celebrate this moment for yourself. Celebration is nurturing and helps you stay in momentum of living the life you desire.

This is still a journey though and it does not stop here. You have opened many doors for yourself in this journaling process and now you get to decide how you want to move forward with it. Our life is created by the choices we make as we co-create our existence with spirit. You have the choice to keep coming back to this truth of your soul and all of its limitless beauty. You can keep building on this and expanding your awareness within that truth.

Self-discovery empowers you and leads you to awareness time and time again. Your power is always in this moment, even if you forgot your truth for the last month, your power is in what you do right now. The energy will build in what you focus on. If you focus on love, you will always find reasons to feel joy. If you focus on pain, you will always find reasons to suffer. That is how powerful you are!

So now you get to decide how you would like journaling to continue to support you throughout your life. It is ok if you take breaks and try new things. This is your process and guilt should never be your driving force. However, you will always have this to come back to at any point in your life. It will always be here as a means of support as you need it.

Your journaling can continue to be a daily practice and it can look different each time. Some days you can simply sit in gratitude and write your moments of joy. Other days you can dump out all the heavy thoughts and ask yourself the deep and transforming questions. You can always come back to this journal to get insight and ideas on which questions to ask or explore for yourself. Remember to ask yourself *Why, How, When,* or *What* to help you dive deeper into exploring your life.

Remember, you are a sacred being who deserves designated time for yourself to feel nurtured and cared for each day. Allow this process to evolve, learn from all of your lessons, and celebrate all of your wins along the way.

Sending you so much love,

Amanda

xo

PS I have a few bonus questions for you to tap into!

What have been my biggest aha moments from this journaling experience?

_____

_____

_____

_____

_____

_____

_____

_____

_____

_____

_____

_____

How do I want to nurture my new awareness?

_____

_____

_____

_____

_____

How would I like to use journaling moving forward?

_____

_____

_____

What do I wish I gained more clarity on during this time?

_____

_____

_____

_____

How can I explore this further to gain the clarity I am looking for?

_____

_____

_____

_____

How will I celebrate all that I have done for myself in this space?

_____

_____

_____

_____

What are the last words I want to write to myself? What do I always want to remember?

_____

_____

_____

_____

_____

_____

_____

_____

_____

_____

_____

_____

Gratitude

Today I am grateful for:

_____

_____

_____

_____

_____

_____

_____

_____

Moments of Joy

Today's moments of joy:

_____

_____

_____

_____

_____

_____

_____

_____

_____

_____

To order more copies of this book, find books by other
Canadian authors, or make inquiries about publishing
your own book, contact PageMaster at:

PageMaster Publication Services Inc.
11340-120 Street, Edmonton, AB T5G 0W5
books@pagemaster.ca
780-425-9303

catalogue and e-commerce store
PageMasterPublishing.ca/Shop

About the Author

Amanda Moser is a Psychic Medium, Intuitive Life Coach, and Reiki Master based out of Saskatchewan, Canada. She has been serving clients all across Canada since 2016. She provides coaching in-person and online, as well as retreats, workshops, and speaking events.

For more information on Amanda's services visit:

www.amandamoser.com

Photo by Brittany Flegel Photography